EARTH EXPLORATIONS

Fossils

JENNY KARPELENIA

PERFECTION LEARNING®

Editorial Director: Susan C. Thies
Editor: Mary L. Bush
Design Director: Randy Messer
Book Design: Tobi S. Cunningham, Michelle J. Glass
Cover Design: Michael A. Aspengren

A special thanks to the following for his
scientific review of the book:
Kristin Mandsager
Instructor of Physics and Astronomy
North Iowa Area Community College

Image Credits:
Associated Press: p. 24; ©Richard Cummins/CORBIS: p. 5 (bottom); ©Jonathan Blair/CORBIS: p. 12;
©Bettmann/CORBIS: p. 21; ©Hulton-Deutsch Collection/CORBIS: p. 22; ©Jonathan Blair/CORBIS:
p. 25; ©Reuters/CORBIS: p. 35; ©Hal Horwitz/CORBIS: p. 41 (bottom); ©Christopher Cormack/CORBIS:
p. 42 (top)

Photos.com: front cover, back cover, Try This! backgrounds, pp. 3, 4, 5 (top), 6, 7, 9, 10, 11 (top),
13 (top & bottom), 14, 15, 19, 26, 27, 28, 32, 33, 34, 36, 37, 40, 42 (bottom), 44; Corel
Professional Photos: pp. 16 (top & bottom), 30–31, 31 (top), 38 (top), 41 (top & middle);
ClipArt.com: pp. 11 (bottom), 20; Photodisc: p. 29; Perfection Learning Corporation: pp. 8, 18;
Michael Aspengren: pp. 23, 31 (bottom); Tobi Cunningham: p. 38 (bottom); Michelle Glass: p. 39

For information, contact
Perfection Learning® Corporation
1000 North Second Avenue, P.O. Box 500
Logan, Iowa 51546-0500.
Phone: 1-800-831-4190
Fax: 1-800-543-2745
perfectionlearning.com

1 2 3 4 5 6 PP 09 08 07 06 05 04
ISBN 0-7891-6253-9

Table of Contents

A Fossil Field Trip

Your teacher has been talking about this field trip for the past two weeks. The day has finally arrived. You've been studying **fossils** in science, and today your class is spending the day at a local history museum. While you're glad to be getting out of school, the thought of spending the day at a museum isn't exactly thrilling. Why couldn't you be going on a field trip to the amusement park instead?

After a bouncy bus ride, you arrive at the museum. You walk from room to room, listening as the tour guide explains the exhibits. First you visit the rocks-and-minerals display and the Native American artifacts. Finally you get to the fossil exhibit. You hate to admit it, but it looks interesting.

Cretaceous shrimp lived 146 million to 65 million years ago.

You wander around the room checking out the various fossils. Leaf imprints decorate rocks. The fossilized snail shell looks just like the live snail in your classroom fish tank. The **trilobite** fossils look like huge bugs covered in armor. You're glad they don't live in your backyard. The fish fossil is nearly perfect. You can see almost every bone in its body. Up ahead are the dinosaurs. The bones of a stegosaurus, triceratops, and tyrannosaurus rex are put together like puzzle pieces. Their size is amazing. The six-inch T. rex teeth send a shiver down your spine.

The triceratops was named for the three (tri) horns on the top of its head.

You can almost imagine what the dinosaurs were like when they were alive. Maybe coming to the museum wasn't such a boring field trip after all.

Viewer Beware!

Many of the dinosaurs found in museums are not fossils. They are actually just replicas of dinosaur fossils made out of fiberglass or resin.

Tyrannosaurus rex skeleton

The albertosaurus was a meat-eating dinosaur that walked on two legs.

What Is a Fossil?

Fossils are the remains of once-living things. Bones, teeth, and shells are fossil remains. Fossils can also be traces, or signs, of past life and activity. Footprints, leaf impressions, and nests are fossilized traces of earlier life. An item usually has to be at least 10,000 years old before it is considered a fossil.

Keichousauruses are small extinct marine reptiles.

Most living things die without becoming fossilized. They rot, are eaten by animals, or get destroyed by too much heat or pressure underground.

Conditions have to be just right for a living thing to turn into a fossil. The object has to have a quick burial in mud, sand, or other materials. Over time, more material, or **sediment**, covers the remains. Usually only the harder parts of a living thing are left at this point. The softer parts have rotted away. After many years, water moving through the sediment seeps into the remaining parts. The minerals in the water replace the chemicals in the body parts, eventually changing the objects into fossils.

Sometimes living things are trapped in other substances and become preserved as fossils. For example, insects and plant pieces have been trapped in hardened tree sap.

Digging Up Fossils

The word *fossil* means "dug up."

Body Fossils

Body fossils form when the actual parts of a living thing become fossilized. The most common animal body fossils are bones, shells, teeth, and claws. A plant leaf can leave an imprint that gets filled in with sediment. When the sediment hardens, a fossil is formed.

Some body fossils form when an animal dies in or near a body of water. Its body is quickly buried by many layers of sediment carried by the water. The soft parts rot away and the harder parts, such as bones, teeth, and claws, are gradually replaced by minerals in the water. Over millions of years, these hard body parts become fossils.

Many body fossils are formed by the mold and cast process. This happens when an object makes an impression that is then filled in with minerals. A snail shell is a good example of this process. When a snail dies, it slowly sinks to the bottom of the ocean. There it is quickly covered with tiny particles of sand or even smaller particles of mud and clay called *silt*. These particles come from rivers that empty into the ocean. The shell is buried in layer after layer of sand and/or silt. The soft parts of the snail rot away. The heavy layers press the particles into rock. The hard snail shell leaves an imprint (mold) in this hardening rock. Minerals dissolved in the water moving through the rock fill in the mold, making a cast. The cast takes the shape of the shell. It is now a fossil of the snail shell.

Plant fossils are often formed this way as well. A leaf or petal is pressed into rock, forming a mold. Sometimes just the imprint remains and hardens into a fossil. Other times, the mold is filled in and becomes a cast fossil.

How do fossils formed under layers of rock or at the bottom of the ocean reach the Earth's surface? Over time, movement within the Earth pushes layers of rock upward. Wind, water, and ice wear away at the surface and fossils are exposed.

Jell-O Fossils

Mold and cast fossils are like making Jell-O. The container you pour the warm liquid Jell-O into is the mold. The dessert you get when the Jell-O cools and "gels" is the cast.

TRY THIS !

Make your own mold and cast body fossil.

Materials

seashell • disk of clay bigger than the shell • plaster of Paris • water
plastic spoon • plastic container (yogurt or margarine containers work well)

Procedure

Press the shell into the clay and gently pull it out. This is a mold fossil. Mix up a small amount of plaster of Paris according to the directions. Carefully pour it into the shell mold. Let it dry overnight. Peel the clay away from the hardened plaster cast and examine your cast fossil of the shell.

Trace Fossils

Trace fossils form when living things leave clues about their existence. Examples of trace fossils are footprints, burrows, tunnels, nests, and teeth marks. Trace fossils help scientists learn about an animal's body and behaviors. For example, the size, depth, and distance between fossilized footprints can give scientists a good idea about an animal's size, weight, and speed. They can also determine whether an animal walked on two or four legs. Teeth marks are usually found in the bones of other animals, so they can provide details about the diet or enemies of an animal. Burrows, tunnels, and nests can give clues about an animal's **habitat** and sleeping and mating behaviors.

Animal droppings are also trace fossils. A coprolite is fossilized dung. By studying coprolites, scientists may be able to get an idea of an animal's habitat, diet, and size. Coprolites as large as 16 inches around have been found, indicating a very large animal. Unfortunately, it is often difficult to tell which animal a coprolite belongs to unless it is found with an actual skeleton.

Finding

Fossils

Now that you know what a fossil is, the next question is where can you find one (besides in a museum, of course). Most fossils are found in sedimentary rocks. Sedimentary rocks are formed when layers of sediment are squeezed together and cemented into rock over millions of years. Plants and animals that were trapped in the sediment layers become part of this rock.

Fossils are more likely to be found in areas of rock where the sediment layers piled up quickly. The process of rotting requires oxygen. When something is buried quickly, there is less oxygen available. Sedimentary rock formed by landslides, earthquakes, sandstorms, and floods often contain many fossils.

Besides sedimentary rocks, fossils can be found in other places. Areas where old oceans, lakes, and sand dunes once existed have layers of sediment that were laid down over long periods of time. Volcanoes can erupt and throw out volcanic ash.

This ash can fall back to the Earth in layers, trapping living things that then become fossilized. Animals can be stuck in **tar pits** and preserved. Areas that were once covered by glaciers can be sites for finding mammoths and other ice age animals that were frozen in the ice.

More recently, scientists have depended on pictures of land taken from space satellites to help them locate fossils. These pictures show areas of exposed rock or other landforms that may contain fossils. Scientists also depend on one another. If an individual or team finds fossils in an area, it is likely that more fossils are nearby waiting to be discovered.

A paleontologist measures a fish fossil found in an open-pit mine in Germany.

Future Fossil Career

Are you interested in finding fossils? Then maybe you should consider a career in **paleontology**. Paleontology is the branch of science that studies early life-forms through fossils.

Fossilized dinosaur egg

Fossils Around the World

Fossils have been found on all of the seven continents. A *Lagerstätten* is a place that is rich in fossils. *Lagerstätten* is a German word meaning "lode place." A lode is a deposit, or amount, of material found in one area. In this case, the lode would be a large number of fossils.

Chengjiang, China, and the Gobi Desert in Asia are known for their rare ancient fossils. Fossil hunters have found a variety of dinosaurs, dinosaur eggs, and even a baby dinosaur inside an egg. **Prehistoric** bird fossils were discovered in the Gobi Desert.

In Solnhofen, Germany, a unique fossil creature was found in limestone. This half-dinosaur, half-bird creature was an archaeopteryx (ar kee AHP tuh riks). It had the body shape and teeth of a reptile, but the feathers and wings of a bird.

The Ediacara Hills of Australia are home to a large collection of ancient soft-bodied organisms. These fossils are more than 500 million years old.

A Lagerstätten found in the Canadian Rockies is the Burgess Shale. Many soft-bodied animals, such as worms and jellyfish, have left their fossils in this shale (hardened mud).

Archaeopteryx fossil

Dinosaur National Monument

Fossils in the United States

Many fossil sites exist in the United States. Dinosaur National Monument is located in Colorado and Utah. It is the richest deposit of dinosaur fossils in the world. This area used to be an old river channel. When dinosaurs died, their bones were swept downstream by the flooding river and were buried by sediment. In 1909, Earl Douglass was the first to find thousands of dinosaur bones in the area. The government has protected this special place since 1915. One wall of the visitors' center is called the Quarry Wall. It is an actual rock layer with many dinosaur bones sticking out of it. Most of the dinosaur fossils found at Dinosaur National Monument were large plant-eating sauropods (SOR uh podz).

The Rancho La Brea Tar Pits in California are a fossil trap. Long ago, animals were caught and buried in the sticky tar. Now when pools of tar rise to the Earth's crust through cracks in the surface, they bring with them the bones of these large prehistoric animals. The fossils of mastodons, camels, giant sloths, American lions, saber-toothed cats, and wolves have all been found in the tar pits.

The farmlands of northeastern Nebraska hide the secrets of ancient life. Underneath the rolling flatlands of the Ashfall Fossil Beds is a volcanic ash bed filled with the remains of rhinoceroses, horses, camels, and birds. Most of the bones found in this area are still joined together because the animals were buried so suddenly by volcanoes.

The Green River Formation is located in parts of Colorado, Utah, and Wyoming. Many fish, reptile, bird, and mammal fossils have been dug up at this site. The fossils found in this area indicate changes in the Earth's environment. Fish fossils show that there were once deep lakes. Plant and animal fossils show that the climate was once warmer and wetter than it is now. For example, fossil crocodiles were found at Green River, and their survival would be difficult in the cooler, drier climate of the states now.

↑ These fish fossils were found at the Green River Formation.

Formation Is Home to the Oldest Flying Mammal

The oldest bat fossil was found at Green River Formation. The bat's whole skeleton was preserved, along with wing membranes.

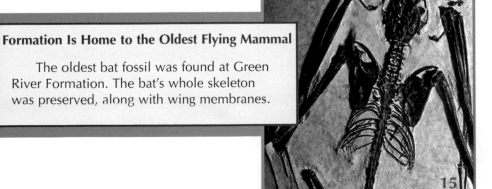

15

The Grand Canyon in Arizona was formed when the Colorado River carved through many layers of sedimentary rock. The rock layers—and the fossils within them—were left exposed. Plant fossils found in the Canyon include ferns and **conifers**. Animal fossils include shelled ocean animals such as clams and snails. Fish, reptiles, amphibians, and even fossilized worm tunnels have been discovered in the layers of rock.

Conifer trees on the north rim of the Grand Canyon

Visitors can hike down through the rock layers of the canyon.

How Old
Is It?

The oldest fossils are approximately 3.5 billion years old. How do scientists know how old these fossils are? And how do they determine the age of a newly found fossil? **Relative dating** and **absolute dating** are two methods used to figure out a fossil's age.

Relative Dating

Relative dating uses rock layers to determine the approximate age of fossils. In general, bottom rock layers were formed first, so they are older than the layers on top. So fossils found in the bottom layers are older than those found in top layers. Fossils found in middle layers are younger than those on the bottom and older than those on top. Relative dating orders fossils from youngest to oldest—it does not provide exact ages.

Absolute Dating

Absolute dating is a way to find a fossil's age in years by testing the rocks surrounding it. Certain **elements** in rocks break down through nuclear decay into other elements. These changing elements are said to be radioactive. Radioactive elements have well-known half-lifes. This is the time it takes for half of the element to decay, or change, into a new element.

Nuclear Decay

In some elements, the nucleus, or center, of an atom in the element can spontaneously turn into an atom of another element. This is called *nuclear decay*.

Some elements have half-lifes of a few thousand years. An example is carbon. A type of carbon called *carbon-14* decays into a different element called *nitrogen-14*. If a sample of carbon was made entirely of carbon-14, in 5730 years, half of the sample will have decayed into nitrogen-14. In another 5730 years, half of the remaining carbon-14 will have turned into nitrogen-14, and so on. This means the half-life of carbon is 5730 years.

Other elements have much longer half-lifes. An example is the element uranium-235. Its half-life is more than 700 million years. In that time, half of the uranium will have begun a series of decays that leads to the final creation of the element lead-207.

How do half-lifes help determine a fossil's age? By figuring out how much of a radioactive element is left in a rock, scientists can use the element's half-life timeline to figure out the rock's age. Any fossils found in the rock are the same age. For example, if half of the uranium-235 in a rock has decayed into lead-207, then the rock is approximately 700 million years old. A fish fossil found in that rock would then also be about 700 million years old.

TRY THIS !

Practice absolute dating with licorice. You will need one long piece of shoestring licorice, a metric ruler, and a butter knife or scissors. Measure the length of the whole licorice piece. This will represent the original amount of a radioactive element. Cut the licorice in half. Eat one half. The piece you ate represents the half-life of the licorice. Half of the radioactive element has now changed into a new element (in your stomach). Now cut the remaining piece in half again. Eat one half. Repeat this process again and again. Keep track of how many times you can do this (how many half-lifes the licorice has). Eventually you will have such a small piece of licorice that you will not be able to cut it in half. Almost all of the radioactive element has now decayed into a new element.

Index Fossils

Index fossils help scientists determine the age of rocks. Some **species** of living things were once very common. Large numbers of them existed before they died out. Scientists look for layers of these fossils in rocks and use them to date the rock. If, for example, fossils known to be 300 million years old are found in a rock layer, then the rock must also be 300 million years old.

Trilobite fossils arc an example of an index fossil. Trilobites were ocean animals with flat, oval bodies. They were common between 545 million and 251 million years ago. Over 1000 different species lived during that time period. Rocks containing trilobites can, therefore, be estimated at 251 million to 545 million years old.

Ammonite fossils were very common 251 million to 65 million years ago. These index fossils were ocean animals with flat spiral shells. They became extinct about 65 million years ago. Ammonite fossils are very useful as a means of dating rocks that formed between 65 million and 251 million years ago.

Marine ammonite

Ammonites

Trilobites

Great Fossil

Hunters

Many curious men, women, and children have found and studied fossils. A paleontologist is a scientist who specializes in fossils. He or she studies fossils to find out clues about the past. Below are just a few of the many paleontologists around the world who have made major discoveries related to fossils.

William Parker Foulke

William Parker Foulke found the first dinosaur in the United States. It was a duck-billed dinosaur named hadrosaurus (HAD ruh sor uhs). Foulke found the fossil in New Jersey in 1838.

Small Discoveries

Even children have done their part in finding important fossils. In 1995, 3-year-old David Schiffler of New Mexico found a dinosaur egg when digging in the ground with his toy backhoe. The same year, 12-year-old Tess Owen found an imprint of a T. rex skin in a rock in Canada. In 1997, a nine-year-old boy found the remains of a woolly mammoth sticking out of the ground near his home in Siberia, Russia.

Mary Anning

Mary Anning grew up in England in the early 1800s. She was fascinated by fossils and shells as a child. She even collected them and sold them to help her family earn money. Anning was the first person to find a fossilized swimming dinosaur known as an ichthyosaurus (IK thee uh sor uhs). She also found many other fossils, including plesiosaurs (PLEE see uh sorz), pterodactyls (tair uh DAK tuhlz), sharks, and other fish and reptiles.

Barnum Brown

Barnum Brown was a dinosaur fossil hunter in the early 1900s. He traveled all over the world collecting fossils. In 1902, Brown found the first tyrannosaurus rex skeleton in Montana.

Barnum Brown works on a model of a dreadnaught, the rarest dinosaur discovered so far.

Charles Walcott

Beginning in 1909, Charles Walcott collected more than 65,000 fossils in the Burgess Shale area of Canada. The amazing thing about these fossils is that they are mostly from animals with soft bodies. Worms, sponges, and other ancient **arthropods** were buried in fast-moving mudfalls in the area.

Roy Andrews

The red sandstone of the Gobi Desert is full of many dinosaur and early mammal skeletons. Roy Andrews made some major discoveries in the Gobi in the 1920s when he was a paleontologist for the American Museum of Natural History. Andrews found a velociraptor (vuh LAH suh rap tor) dinosaur skeleton and a fossilized nest. He was also the first to find fossilized dinosaur eggs. His discoveries in the Gobi have led many other paleontologists to continue searching the desert for fossils.

Roy Andrews examines dinosaur eggs found in Mongolia.

Luis and Walter Alvarez

Luis and Walter Alvarez are a father and son team of scientists. The men worked together on a theory of dinosaur **extinction**. The Alvarez men believe that a huge rock from outer space called a *meteorite* hit the planet about 65 million years ago. All of the plants and animals in the nearby area were killed by the blast. The massive impact of the meteorite caused fires, huge waves (tsunamis), and volcanic eruptions. Dust in the air blocked out the Sun, and the temperature on Earth dropped. The plants and animals of the time could not adjust to the new conditions, so they died out.

A crater made from a meteorite during the right time period has been discovered buried under sea sediment off the Yucatan Peninsula. This, along with other evidence, supports the Alvarezes' beliefs. Their theory, known as the K-T extinction, is widely accepted today.

Ruth Mason

When she was seven years old, Ruth Mason found a huge bed of dinosaur fossils on her family's ranch in South Dakota. Since then, hundreds of dinosaur bones and teeth have been found nearby at what is now called the Ruth Mason Quarry. Many of the fossils belong to duck-billed, plant-eating dinosaurs.

Robert Bakker

Robert Bakker is a well-known paleontologist and dinosaur artist. Many of his theories are controversial. For instance, he believes that some dinosaurs were not cold-blooded reptiles but warm-blooded animals related to birds. Bakker currently studies dinosaur habitats. He is also comparing the skulls of some plant-eating dinosaurs to prove his theory that they may have communicated by sounds made in their skulls.

> **Jurassic Park Pointers from a Paleontologist**
>
> Robert Bakker was a consultant for the popular dinosaur movie *Jurassic Park.*

William Hammer

William Hammer is a paleontologist who found the first dinosaur fossil in Antarctica. In 1990, Dr. Hammer found a frozen cryolophosaurus (creye uh LOF uh sor uhs) fossil. The cryolophosaurus was a dinosaur with a large crest on the top of its head. The fossil is about 200 million years old. Dr. Hammer's discovery proves that Antarctica has not always been as cold as it is now. Dr. Hammer has also found other meat-eating dinosaurs and a flying reptile called a pterosaur (TAIR uh sor) in the Antarctic as well.

Susan Hendrickson

Susan Hendrickson has a fossilized T. rex named after her. In 1990, Hendrickson found the world's biggest, heaviest, and most complete T. rex skeleton in the badlands of South Dakota. More than 200

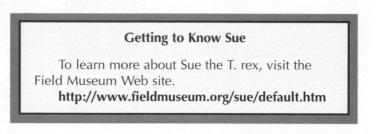

Getting to Know Sue

To learn more about Sue the T. rex, visit the Field Museum Web site.
http://www.fieldmuseum.org/sue/default.htm

bones of the skeleton were found. Sue the T. rex is now on display at the Field Museum in Chicago, Illinois.

Sue has 58 huge teeth. These teeth were made for grabbing and piercing food. When teeth broke off, new teeth would take their place.

Plant Fossils

Early Organisms Lead to Plant Life

Scientists believe the Earth is about 4.6 billion years old. In its first billion years, the planet remained lifeless. Conditions were too harsh for even the simplest life-forms. Eventually the first **organisms,** archea and cyanobacteria, appeared. Cyanobacteria were the first life-forms to use the energy from the Sun to make their own food. Their bodies could not use the oxygen produced in the process, so they released it into the atmosphere. With more oxygen available, the growth of other life-forms became possible.

Colonies of Cyanobacteria

Stromatolites are fossilized colonies of cyanobacteria. Many of these ancient bacteria were found in Australia. Stromatolites look like stony mounds. Some can grow as tall as 19 feet.

A geologist examines stromatolites in the Caribbean Sea.

Plants have lived on Earth longer than animals. Fossil evidence has led to the belief that plants lived in the ocean first before moving to land about 400 million years ago. Older fossils show that plants were once better suited to life in the water. Younger plant fossils show adaptations to life on land, such as woody stems to draw up water from the ground and waterproof outer layers to prevent drying out.

Prehistoric fossils have shown that some of the earliest land plants were club mosses, ferns, and horsetails. Forests of these early plants grew when the dinosaurs roamed the Earth. Conifers, **cycads**, and gingkos are other common ancient plant fossils. Flowering plant fossils appeared later. They were followed by younger grass fossils that are only 50 million years old.

Plant Paleontology

Paleobotanists are scientists who study plant fossils. They examine features of these fossils to piece together the history and habitats of ancient plant life.

Gingko leaves

Cycad leaves

Leaf Imprints

One common plant fossil is a leaf imprint. When a leaf dies and settles at the bottom of a lake or pond, it begins to rot. As it breaks down, the leaf may leave imprints in the mud. Over millions of years, the mud is sandwiched between layers of sediment and hardens into sedimentary rock. The leaf imprint is then fossilized in the rock.

Paleobotanists study the shape and size of leaf imprints to determine what types of plant they came from. They can also get an idea of plant environments from leaf imprints. For example, large, smooth, curved leaves may indicate that a plant grew in a tropical climate. Smaller, pointed, jagged leaf ends may show that the plant grew in a cooler, drier climate.

Petrified Wood

Fossilized wood is called *petrified wood*. Petrified wood has turned to stone. When trees or other plants die and fall to the floor of a forest, lake, or swamp, they can be buried by sediment before rotting. Over millions of years, the plant material becomes compressed within sedimentary rock. Water fills in spaces in the wood of plant stems or tree trunks. Minerals in the water, such as silica and quartz, gradually replace the wood, turning it to stone. Often these minerals will form colorful petrified wood in shades of blues, reds, purples, pinks, oranges, and greens.

Petrified Forest National Park in northern Arizona is an awesome display of petrified wood. Fallen logs from ancient conifer trees are scattered across the park. Some of them are more than 100 feet long and 10 feet in diameter. The park is also home to the Painted Desert. This is an area of exposed sedimentary rock. Minerals in the rock layers give the land its "painted" look. Many fossils have been found in this colorful sedimentary rock.

Erupting Sediment

Often a volcanic eruption is the cause of sudden plant death. When a volcano erupts, volcanic ash covers trees and other plants in the area. Petrified wood is often the result of this quick burial in volcanic ash.

Animal

Fossils

Paleobiologists study animal fossils. The size and shape of fossils such as bones, teeth, and shells give a paleobiologist clues to an animal's size and shape when it was alive. Fossils may also provide hints about how an animal moved or behaved. The location of fossils can indicate an animal's habitat.

Insects

Insect fossils have told paleobiologists much about the past life of bugs. Insects were some of the first animals to live on land. The oldest insect fossils are about 400 million years old. These early insects could not fly. It wasn't until about 325 million years ago that some species began to develop wings.

Without many predators around, some prehistoric insects grew to be huge in size. Some dragonfly species had wingspans of up to 30 inches. Larger predators, climate changes, and available food supply may all have contributed to the extinction of these giant insects.

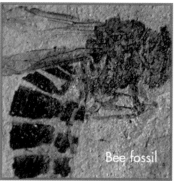
Bee fossil

Damsel fly fossil

Over time, insects **adapted** to new environments, and today, nearly one million species of insects exist in different habitats. In fact, there are more insect species than all species of other living things combined.

Insects do not have bones to leave behind as fossils. They do have a crunchy outer layer called an *exoskeleton* that can leave imprints in rocks. Sometimes insects are preserved in amber. Amber is fossilized tree sap from ancient pine trees. Insects or small animals become caught in the sticky sap and fossilize as it hardens. Perfect insect specimens have been protected in a coating of amber.

Ocean Animals

Ocean animal fossils include reptiles and amphibians, shelled animals such as snails and clams, and many species of fish. Turtle and crocodile fossils from millions of years ago show that these creatures were similar to today's reptiles. Sharks and other fish have left behind very detailed bones, teeth, and imprints. In one rare case, the fossil of a small fish was found inside the fossil of a larger fish. Amazingly, the larger fish was buried in sediment before his dinner could be digested!

TRY THIS!

Make your own amber insect fossils. Gather a box of yellow Jell-O, two ice cube trays, a bag of gummy bugs, and a can of cooking spray. Spray the ice cube trays. Mix up the Jell-O according to the directions on the box. Pour it into the ice cube trays and refrigerate. When the Jell-O is starting to get firm, place a gummy bug in each cube. Let the Jell-O set completely. When it is set, release the "amber" and check out the fossil insects inside.

Crab fossil

Ammonites, trilobites, and swimming dinosaurs are now extinct, but they've left behind many fossils to tell the tales of their lives. Ammonites are extinct shelled ocean animals related to octopus and squid. The ammonite shell was tightly coiled and divided into chambers. These creatures could live more than 300 feet deep in the ocean. One reason they are believed to have become extinct was a climate change that caused many of the world's oceans to become shallow or dry up.

Trilobites were named for their appearance. Two lines running down their backs made the animal appear to have three (tri) lobes, or sections. These animals lived in the ocean and breathed through gills. They did not have a backbone. They did have a hard outer skeleton and jointed limbs, similar to a crab or an insect. Trilobites were usually between 1.2 and 4 inches long but could grow as large as 40 inches. The disappearance of bodies of seawater were most likely responsible for the trilobites' extinction.

Swimming reptiles, such as plesiosaurs, mosasaurs (MOH zuh sorz), and nothosaurs (NAH thuh sorz), also left fossils behind. Their streamlined bodies were designed for the water, with flipperlike paddles and sharp teeth for eating fish, turtles, and other prey.

Plesiosaurus means "near lizard."

Land Animals

Many interesting animals once roamed the Earth. Dinosaurs, woolly rhinos, woolly mammoths, mastodons, saber-toothed cats, and giant deer are just a few of these unique creatures.

Over 500 different types of dinosaur fossils have been found. Paleobiologists study dinosaur bones and compare them to the bones of modern-day animals. The size, shape, and position of bones can tell scientists a lot about prehistoric animals and their relationship to today's animals. For example, the straight, sturdy legs of the huge apatosaurus (uh pah tuh SOR us) and a modern-day elephant are similar, so it is believed that the apatosaurus plodded slowly like an elephant does.

Saber-toothed tiger

About 100 fossilized woolly mammoths have been found in the world so far. Most of these have been in the muddy ice of Canada and Russia. Woolly mammoths lived from about 2 million years ago until about 10,000 years ago. They died out with the end of the last ice age. Scientists believe they might have died out due to the climate change or overhunting and habitat destruction by people.

The Return of the Mammoth?

Scientists have collected **DNA** from a woolly mammoth that was found frozen in Siberia. Some scientists believe that perhaps someday a mammoth might be cloned.

Human skull fossil

Humans

Paleoanthropologists study fossils of ancient humans and their artifacts, such as tools and weapons. The skeletons of early human forms provide much information about prehistoric life on Earth. Ancient tools and weapons show the development of humans as warriors, hunters, farmers, and inventors.

The oldest-known human (Homo sapiens) fossil is 160,000 years old. Older humanlike fossils have been found, but they are not of the same species as today's humans. Some of the early humanlike ancestors were called Homo habilis, Homo erectus, and Neanderthal man (Homo sapiens neanderthalensis). Their ages range from several hundred thousand years old to a few million years old.

Is It Getting Old?

Are you starting to notice a pattern in the words that deal with the science of fossils? The prefix *paleo-* found in *paleontology, paleontologist, paleobiologist, paleobotanist,* and *paleoanthropologist* comes from a Greek word meaning "ancient" or "long ago." So scientists in the "paleo" fields study ancient things or things from long ago—otherwise known as fossils. Just imagine how "old" everything in their lives must be!

Living

Fossils

Living fossils are certain species that have not changed significantly in many millions of years. Some animals and plants that are living now look the same as fossils of those species from millions of years ago. More than 500 living fossils have been recorded. Examples of living fossils include gingko trees, crocodiles, horseshoe crabs, cockroaches, and coelacanths.

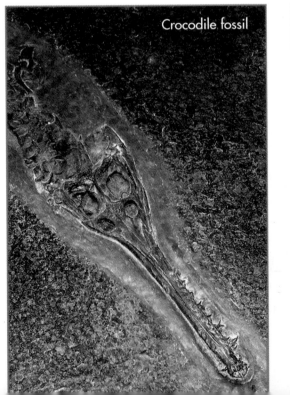

Crocodile fossil

Coelacanth

Horseshoe crabs

Gingko Trees

Dinosaurs may have munched on gingko leaves more than 200 million years ago. These large trees have changed very little in all those years. The leaf shape of the gingko has changed slightly over time. Long ago, the leaves were divided into sections, or lobes. In modern trees, the lobes have joined to form leaves that look like fans. Medicines made from gingko trees are believed to improve concentration and memory.

Name Tag for a Tree

Gingko trees are also called *maidenhair trees*.

Crocodiles

Crocodiles have lived for more than 200 million years. These animals have several characteristics that have enabled them to adapt and survive without much change. Crocodiles are strong creatures with a tough skin that protects them from injury. They are also not picky eaters. If one food source runs out, they can easily find a different one.

Horseshoe Crabs

A 430-million-year-old fossil of a horseshoe crab revealed that these animals were much the same as today's crabs. These living fossils have a hard outer shell that protects the soft body inside. Horseshoe crabs can handle extreme conditions. They can go without eating for a year and can handle icy cold ocean temperatures or a very high salt content in oceans.

Cockroaches

Cockroaches have survived unchanged for about 350 million years. These insects are found all over the world. They can live in any type of climate or environment—including your kitchen cupboards! Cockroaches can also eat almost anything. These adaptations have made them very successful throughout time.

Coelacanths

Coelacanths (SEE luh kanths) are fish that first appeared on Earth around 400 million years ago. At one time, 120 different varieties of coelacanths existed. After the dinosaurs died out about 65 million years ago, the coelacanth was believed to have been extinct as well. Then in 1938, a healthy, living coelacanth was discovered in the Indian Ocean off the coast of South Africa. This species of coelacanths are blue fish that eat squid, eels, and other fish. They have four stubby lower fins, spiny scales, and a pronged tip on their tail just like their ancient relatives. In the 1990s, a second species of brown coelancanths were found as well.

Old Fourlegs

The coelacanth was nicknamed "Old Fourlegs" because of its unique leglike fins. At one time, it was believed that the fish actually crawled along the ocean floor on these fins. Now scientists know that the short, stubby fins are used for quick swimming movement.

Fossil Fuels

Coal

You know that fossils teach about past life on Earth. But did you know that fossils also keep you warm and run your TV, computer, and stereo? **Fossil fuels** are fuels made from the remains of prehistoric plants and animals. Coal, oil, and natural gas are fossil fuels.

How Does It Work?

When plants are alive, they trap the Sun's energy in their green leaves. They use that energy, along with water and carbon dioxide, to produce the food they need to live. The process of this energy change is called *photosynthesis.*

Millions of years later, those same plants may become fossils. Burning them releases the energy as heat. That heat can be used to warm schools, homes, and businesses. Some furnaces burn natural gas. Others run on electricity, which can be created from the burning of fossil fuels. That electricity is also used to power all the electrical devices in your world, including entertainment systems, blow-dryers, washing machines, stoves, and dishwashers.

Coal

Swamp plants from millions of years ago became coal because there was little oxygen to help them rot. Instead, the weight of upper layers of sediment and partially decayed plants compressed the plants together. The water was squeezed out, and over time, different types of coal were formed.

Where Did All the Oxygen Go?

Swamps contain low amounts of oxygen because the water doesn't flow and mix with air. Bacteria and plants use up the oxygen originally dissolved in the water, and it isn't replaced with oxygen from the air. It's like a fish tank. Without a machine (aerator) to bubble air through the water in the tank, the fish would use up the oxygen and die.

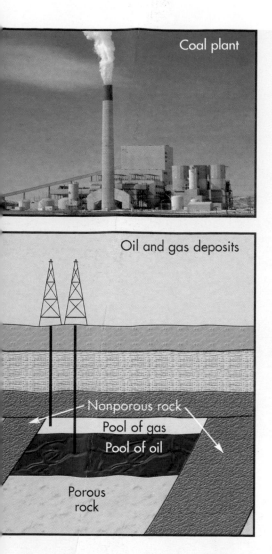

Coal plant

Oil and gas deposits

Nonporous rock
Pool of gas
Pool of oil

Porous
rock

Today, most coal is used to supply energy to electric companies. In fact, electric companies use more than four-fifths of the coal mined in the United States. These companies burn coal to run giant fan blades called *turbines*, which generate electricity.

Oil and Natural Gas

Oil and natural gas are made from the remains of plankton. Plankton is formed when tiny plants and animals settle on sea floors when they die and are buried by layers of mud and sand. Over thousands of years, heat and pressure change the plankton layer into a thick black liquid called *oil*. Higher amounts of heat and pressure will cause a natural gas deposit to form.

Oil and gas are pumped to the Earth's surface and burned to release heat energy. Oil, also known as petroleum, can be processed and turned into other products, such as gasoline, plastic, candles, crayons, and lip balm.

Disappearing Fossil Fuels

Fossil fuels are a nonrenewable resource. This means that they will run out someday. Humans are digging them out of the ground much faster than they are being replaced. Remember, it takes millions of years for fossil fuels to form. Many scientists are working on solutions to this problem. They are trying to come up with easy-to-use, affordable, renewable sources of energy. Wind, solar, water, and **geothermal** energy are alternatives to fossil fuels.

The Future of

Fossils

Changing with the Times

The Earth has changed greatly since its formation 4.6 billion years ago. All living organisms on the planet have changed throughout this time period as well. Fossils support this idea of change, or **evolution**.

One theory supported by fossils is continental drift. This idea was developed by Alfred Wegener in 1915. Wegener believed that the Earth's landmasses were once joined in one huge continent called Pangaea.

Then, approximately 130 million years ago, the continent broke up into smaller pieces that have since been slowly drifting around on the surface of the Earth.

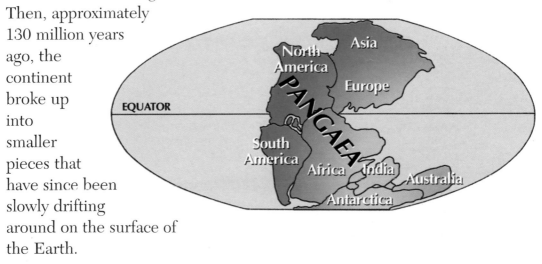

Although many scientists did not believe Wegener's idea at first, fossil evidence does support his theory. Plant and animal fossils have been found in places where they could not have existed on today's continents. For example, a plant called a *glossopteris* was an ancient fern tree. Its fossils have been found in many places in the world, such as South America, southern Africa, India, and even Antarctica. However, a glossopteris was a tropical plant. It could not grow in today's cold Antarctic climate. But if a glossopteris first grew near the equator on Pangaea and was fossilized there, it could have been carried to new locations when the supercontinent broke up into smaller pieces.

Fossils are also evidence of Charles Darwin's theory of evolution. Darwin believed that living things adapt to their changing environment in order to survive. Those species that adapt most successfully will survive and those that don't will die off. Fossils have proven that as the climate or environment changed over time, living things changed as well.

Charles Darwin

Survival of the Fittest

Darwin's theory of evolution also became known as "survival of the fittest." This means that species that fit best in an environment survive to produce offspring while those that are not suited to the conditions become extinct.

Stegosaurus

Velociraptor

Going, Going, Gone

Out of all the animals and plants that have ever lived on Earth, only about one percent are alive today. Ninety-nine percent of all species are now extinct.

Fossils provide evidence of species extinction. Dinosaurs, woolly mammoths, and mastodons are a few extinct animal species. Fossils of huge fast-growing ferns, scale trees, and giant scouring rushes are proof of extinct prehistoric plants. Many other animals and plants once existed but are now gone forever. Fortunately, they left their fossils behind as testimony of their existence.

Throughout time, several mass extinctions have occurred. Huge numbers of living things were wiped out over a few million years. (A million years may sound like a long time, but it is a short period in the Earth's timeline.) By analyzing fossils from different time periods, scientists have determined that there were five mass extinctions. All five of these extinctions are thought to have been the result of natural causes, such as meteorites and climate changes.

Plants That Clean Pots?

Scouring rushes are tall evergreen plants with thin, hollow, round stems. Tiny leaves grow in rings around the stems. Scouring rushes were abundant 360 million–250 million years ago. Today, only a few species remain. Rushes have an abrasive material in their stems that makes them useful for scouring (cleaning) cooking utensils and polishing furniture.

Many of the world's current scientists are concerned that we are in a sixth time of mass extinction. Species of plants and animals are becoming extinct today at a faster rate than ever before. According to the famous paleoanthropologist Richard Leakey, between 17,000 and 100,000 species are disappearing every year. At that speed, about half of the Earth's species will be extinct in the next 100 years. And this time, natural causes are not to blame. People are to blame. People who destroy habitats, overhunt, pollute the air and water, and use up nonrenewable resources

Richard Leakey

are contributing to the mass extinction of many plant and animal species. If the Earth does indeed suffer a sixth mass extinction, its citizens may have only themselves to blame.

❖ ❖ ❖ ❖ ❖

From evolution to extinction, fossils have provided key information to understanding the past and the present. It is up to the human species to ensure that today's living things don't become tomorrow's fossils.

Internet Connections and Related Reading for Fossils

http://www.enchantedlearning.com/subjects/dinosaurs/
The table of contents at this site will lead you to information on dinosaurs, evolution/extinction, and fossils. Click on any of the numerous topics for easy-to-understand facts and fun.

http://www.museum.vic.gov.au/prehistoric/time/index.html
What other fossils exist besides those of dinosaurs? Check out this site for facts on other prehistoric fossils, such as insects, trilobites, and sea stars.

http://www.museum.vic.gov.au/prehistoric/time/plant.html
Explore prehistoric plant fossils, including conifers, gingkos, and ferns.

http://www.well.com/user/davidu/extinction.html
This collection of articles on mass extinction will never run out (unlike the plant and animal life on Earth!).

❖ ❖ ❖ ❖ ❖

Charles Darwin: And the Evolution Revolution by Rebecca Stefoff. This biography of Charles Darwin explores the scientist, his theories, his time, and his impact. Oxford University Press, 1998. [RL 7 IL 6–12] (5481601 PB)

Dinosaur Detectives based on the original series by Joanna Cole. Ms. Frizzle takes her students to the Museum of Natural History to study dinosaurs, but they end up traveling through time to the actual Mesozoic era and coming face-to-face with real meat eaters. Scholastic, 2002. [RL 2.8 IL 2–5] (3372601 PB 3372602 CC)

Dinosaur Hunters by Kate McMullan. Text and illustrations describe what fossils can tell us about dinosaurs and what exciting discoveries the most famous dinosaur hunters have made. Random House, 1989. [RL 3 IL 2–5] (8957401 PB 8957402 CC)

Evolution by Linda Gamlin. An Eyewitness Science Book on evolution. Dorling Kindersley, 1993. [RL 8.3 IL 3–8] (5868706 HB)

Evolution by Alvin and Virginia Silverstein and Laura Silverstein Nunn. Explains a fundamental concept of science, gives some background, and discusses current applications and developments. Millbrook Press, 1998. [RL 5 IL 5–8] (112006 HB)

Extinct! Creatures of the Past by Mary Batten. Describes giant bugs, birds, and mammals that lived long ago and became extinct during the last ice age, discusses the extinction of more recent animals, and examines the effort to protect endangered species. Golden Books, 2000. [RL 2.8 IL 2–4] (3267001 PB 3267002 CC)

Fossil by Paul D. Taylor. An Eyewitness Book on fossils. Dorling Kindersley, 1990. [RL 6.6 IL 5–9] (5865206 HB)

The Fossil Girl: Mary Anning's Dinosaur Discovery by Catherine Brighton. In 1810, 11-year-old Mary Anning and her brother Joe discover a large bony head sticking out of the cliff face. Mary risks her life to make one of the great scientific discoveries of the century. Millbrook Press, 1999. [RL 2.8 IL K–5] (3100706 HB)

Mary Anning: Fossil Hunter by Sally M. Walker. This book describes the life of Mary Anning, who discovered many of the best and most complete fossils in 19th-century England yet received little credit for her work. Lerner, 2001. [RL 3.5 IL K–5] (3348806 HB)

- RL = Reading Level
- IL = Interest Level

Perfection Learning's catalog numbers are included for your ordering convenience. PB indicates paperback. CC indicates Cover Craft. HB indicates hardback.

The pleurosaurus was known as the "sea lizard" because it had a long tail used for swimming and short legs used for walking on land.

Glossary

absolute dating
(AB suh loot DAY ting) process of using the half-life of elements to determine the age of a rock fossil (see separate entry for *element*)

adapt
(uh DAPT) to change characteristics or behaviors in order to survive in a certain environment

arthropod
(AR thruh pahd) animal without a backbone that has joined limbs, a segmented body, and a tough outer exoskeleton or casing

body fossil
(BAH dee FAH suhl) fossil formed when parts of a living thing become fossilized

conifer
(KON uh fer) tree that produces cones; most are evergreens with needles

cycad
(SEYE kuhd) tropical tree with a thick trunk, cones, and sharp pointed leaves like a palm tree

DNA
(dee en ay) material in an organism that passes on traits, or characteristics, from parents to children; deoxyribonucleic acid (see separate entry for *organism*)

element
(EL uh ment) nonliving material made up of one type of atom or particle

evolution
(ev uh LOO shuhn) process by which species change over time

extinction
(ex STINK shuhn) death of all the members of a plant or animal species (see separate entry for *species*)

fossil
(FAH suhl) hardened remains of a plant or animal

fossil fuel
(FAH suhl fyoul) fuel formed from the remains of living things

geothermal	(gee oh THER muhl) type of heat energy produced inside the Earth
habitat	(HAB i tat) place where a plant or animal lives
index fossil	(IN deks FAH suhl) common fossil used to determine the age of rocks
living fossil	(LIV ing FAH suhl) species that hasn't changed significantly in millions of years
organism	(OR guh niz uhm) living thing
paleontology	(pay lee ahn TAH luh jee) study of early life forms using fossils
prehistoric	(pree his STOR ik) related to the period of time before history was recorded in writing
relative dating	(REL uh tiv DAY ting) method of comparing the ages of fossils using the position of rock layers
sediment	(SED uh ment) small pieces of rocks, minerals, shells, and soil
species	(SPEE shees) group of living things that are like one another
tar pit	(tar pit) area where tar naturally accumulates, trapping animals and preserving their bones (tar is a thick black liquid formed from materials such as wood or coal)
trace fossil	(trace FAH suhl) fossilized impression or structure in sedimentary rock that came from the activity of a plant or animal
trilobite	(TREYE luh beyet) extinct ocean arthropod with a segmented body and three lobes (see separate entry for *arthropod*)

Index